The ENCHIRIDION

EPICTETUS

ADAPTED FOR THE CONTEMPORARY
READER BY JAMES HARRIS

ISBN: 9781521308868

COPYRIGHT © 2017 JAMES HARRIS
ALL RIGHTS RESERVED

1	7
2	9
3	11
4	13
5	15
6	17
7	19
8	21
9	23
10	25
11	27
12	29
13	31
14	33
15	35
16	37

17	**39**
18	**41**
19	**43**
20	**45**
21	**47**
22	**49**
23	**51**
24	**53**
25	**56**
26	**58**
27	**60**
28	**62**
29	**64**
30	**68**
31	**70**
32	**72**

33	74
34	80
35	82
36	84
37	86
38	88
39	90
40	92
41	94
42	96
43	98
44	100
45	102
46	104
47	106
48	108

49	110
50	112
51	114

1

There are things within our power, and there are things beyond our power. Within our power are our opinion, aim, desire, dislikes, and, in summary, whatever is our own. Beyond our power is property, reputation, duties, and, in summary, whatever is not ours.

The things within our power are naturally free, unrestricted, unhindered; but those beyond our power are weak, dependent and restricted. So remember if you attribute freedom to things which are not naturally ours and take what belongs to others for yourself, you will be hindered, you will feel sorrow, you will be disturbed, you will then find fault with god and with men. But if you take only those things which are truly your own and view what belongs to others as it really is, then no one can control you, no one can restrict you; you will find fault with no one, you will accuse no one, you will do nothing against your own will; no one will hurt you, you will have no enemies, and you won't suffer any harm.

Therefore, aim at great things such as these, remember that you can't allow yourself any inclination toward the attainment of that which is not yours; and you must quit some of these pursuits, and for the present postpone the rest. But if you already have these, and possess power and wealth, you may miss what true wealth is seeking the power, and you will fail to find that which creates happiness and freedom.

Therefore, begin by being able to say to every unpleasing resemblance, "You are only a resemblance of truth and are not the real thing." And then examine, using the rules you have; but first by this: whether it concerns the things which are within our own power or those which are not; and if it concerns anything beyond our power, be prepared to say that it is not something you require.

2

Remember that any desire we have encourages us to obtain the object of our desire; and anything we dislike we aim to avoid. When someone fails to obtain the object of his desires he becomes disappointed; and if he is subject to something that he dislikes he is unfortunate. If then, you decide to avoid the things you dislike which you can control, you will never suffer any grief from anything in your power to avoid; but if you try to avoid sickness, or death, or poverty, you will run the risk of being unhappy. So we should remove the habit of avoidance from all things that are not within our power, and apply it to things which are undesirable and which are within our power. But for the present, completely restrain desire; because if you desire any of the things not within our own power, you will eventually be disappointed; and we can't even be sure of the things which are within our power. So it is basically a necessity for us not to pursue or to avoid anything, however this must be done with discretion, gentleness and moderation.

3

In regards to anything which delights your mind or is something you really enjoy using or is loved, remind yourself the nature of what they are, beginning with the simplest of things: if you have a favourite mug, remember is just a cup which you like so much—and then, if it is broken, you can bear it; and in the same manner if you view your child or your wife, as a mortal— if either of them dies, you can bear it.

4

When you chose to take any action, remind yourself what is nature of this action. If you are going to the swimming pool, remind yourself of the usual incidents in the pool—some people getting out, others going in, some stealing from the bags left on the side. If you are able to contemplate this, you will be able to go about this action in a safer manner, especially If you can say to yourself, "Now I'm going to the pool and I will keep my own will in harmony with nature." And this should also be used in regards to every other action of ours. Using this, if anything happens during your time in the pool, you will be able to say, "It wasn't just a swim which I desired, but to keep my will in harmony with nature; and won't keep it in harmony if I am out of sync with things which can potentially happen."

5

Men aren't disturbed by reality, but by the view which they take of it. Death is nothing terrible, otherwise it would have appeared to be to Socrates. But terror consists in our idea of death, the idea that death is terrible. When, therefore, we are hindered or disturbed, or in fear, we shouldn't attribute it to others, but to ourselves—that it is purely our own views on the situation. It is the action of an uneducated man to blame others for his own misfortune; but a man who enters education of this kind, will blame himself; and a man perfected, will blame neither himself or others.

6

Don't be happy due to any excellence which is not your own. If a horse were happy, and said, "I'm handsome," it might be accepted. But when you are happy and say, "I have a handsome horse," know that you are happy only on the merit of the horse. What is your own then? This is the use of existence for happiness and not for that which is derived from the inside. So when you are in harmony with nature in this respect, you should be happy due to this reason; that you are happy due to some good of your own.

7

After a voyage, when the ship is anchored, if you go on the shore to get water, you might amuse yourself picking up shellfish or truffle on your way, but your thoughts be on the ship, and perpetually attentive, in case the captain calls, and then you have to leave all these things behind, because they be carried on board the vessel. We are bound like a sheep; likewise, in life. If, instead of truffle or shellfish, you have been granted a wife or a child, there is no objection; but if the captain calls, run to the ship, leave all these things, and never look behind you. But if you are old, never go far from the ship, in case you are missing when called for.

8

Don't demand that events have to happen as you want them to; but wish them to happen as they happen to, and you will go on well.

9

Sickness is an impediment to the body, but not to the will unless you chose it to be. Just as cramp is an impediment to the leg, it isn't to the will; so say this to yourself in regards to everything that happens. Because you will find things to be impediments to something else, but not truly to yourself.

10

When anything occurs, remember to turn to yourself and ask what is required in this situation. If you encounter a handsome person, you will find continence is needed; if pain, then fortitude; if criticism, then patience. And when this is ingrained as a habit, none of these phenomena will have the power to overwhelm you.

11

Never say, "I have lost it," say, "I have restored it." Has your child died? It is restored. Has your wife died? She is restored. Has your estate been taken away? That also has been restored. "But it was a bad man who took it." What does it matter to whose hands took it back? Remember one allowed you to possess it, and hold it as something which was not your own, just like a traveller at the holiday inn.

12

If you want to improve yourself, put to the side reasoning like this: "If I neglect my affairs, I won't be able to do maintenance." But it's better to die from hunger, exempt from grief and fear, than to live in affluence with a disturbed mind. It is better to neglect if it makes you happy.

Therefore, begin with little things. Has a little oil been spilled or a little wine stolen? Say to yourself, "This is the price I pay for peace and tranquillity; and nothing is to be had for nothing."

13

If you want to improve, be content to be viewed by others as foolish and dull with regard to the external. Don't desire to be thought of as a man who knows much; and although you appear to others to be somebody who does, distrust yourself. Be assured, it is not easy at all to keep your will in harmony with nature and to secure external objects; because while you are absorbed in one, you must of necessity neglect another.

14

If you want your children and your wife and your friends to live forever, you are foolish, because you wish for things to be in your power which are not, this is the same as wanting what belongs to others to be your own. So likewise, if you want your maid to be without fault, you are foolish, this is like wishing vice not to be vice but something else. However, if you don't want to be disappointed in your desires, this is in your own power. Exercise, therefore, what is in your power. A man's master is the one who is able to give or remove whatever that man seeks or dislikes. Whoever then who wants to be free, he should wish for nothing, and he should decline nothing which depends on others; or else he can only be a slave.

15

Remember that you should behave at a dinner. When anything is brought around to you put your hand out and take a moderate share. Did it pass by? Don't stop it. Is it yet to come? Don't yearn in desire for it, but wait until it reaches you. And use this manner in regards to children, wife, work, riches; and one day you will be worthy to have dinner with the gods. And if you don't desire to take the things which are placed in front of you, and are even able to forego them, then you will not only be worthy to dine with the gods, but to rule with them also. Because, by doing this, Diogenes and Heraclitus, and others like them, rightly became divine, and were well recognized.

16

When you see anyone crying that his son has left the country or that he has suffered in some way or other, be careful not to be overcome by the apparent evil, but discriminate against it and be ready to say, "What hurts this man is not the occurrence itself—because another man might not be hurt by it—he is hurt by the view he chooses to take of it." As far as conversation goes, however, don't feel the need to accommodate yourself to him and, if you need too, cry with him. Take care, however, not to cry inwardly, too.

17

Remember that you are an actor in a drama of which the supreme creator chooses—if short, then in a short one; if long, then in a long one. If it pleases him that you act as a poor man, or a cripple, or a ruler, or a private citizen, make sure you act it well. Because this is your business—to act well the part given to you, and not to choose the part which belongs to another.

18

When a raven happens to croak unluckily, Don't be overcome by appearances, but discriminate against them and say, "Nothing is a sign to *me*, either to my body, or property, or reputation, or children, or wife. But to *me* all signs are lucky if I say they are. So whatever happens, it is in my power to derive advantage from it."

19

You can be unconquerable if you don't enter into combat which it is not in your power to conquer. When, therefore, you see anyone respected with honours or power, or in high esteem, take care not to be confused by appearances and to declare that he's happy; because if the essence of good consists in things within our own power, there will be no room for envy or emulation. So, in your life, don't desire to be a general, or a senator, or a consul, but to be free; and the only way to do this is to disregard things which lie not within our own power.

20

Remember it's not the person who gives abuse or blows, who insults, but the view we take of these things as insulting. When, therefore, anyone provokes you, be assured that it is your own opinion which provokes you. Therefore, first you should try not to be confused by appearances. Because if you can gain time and rest, you will begin to easily command yourself.

21

Let death and exile, and all other terrible things appear before your eyes daily, but most importantly death; and you will never again entertain a hopeless thought, or too eagerly desire anything.

22

If you really desire to study philosophy, prepare yourself from the beginning to have the majority of people laugh at you and say, "He has now become a philosopher"; and, "He has returned with this arrogant look" In your case, it's best not to have an arrogant look indeed, but be stubborn to maintain the things which appear best to you, like one who was appointed by God to these particular causes. Remember that, if you are persistent, those very people who at first ridiculed you, will afterwards admire you. But if you are conquered by them, and put off, you will be ridiculed twice.

23

If you happen to turn your attention to the external, because you require the pleasure of anyone, you can be assured that you have ruined your scheme of life. Be content, then, in everything, with being a philosopher; and if you wish to appear like this to anyone, first you must appear like this to yourself, and this will suffice.

24

Don't be anxious and let considerations like these distress you: "I will live discredited and be a nobody everywhere." Because discredit is only evil, if you are involved in evil through bad deeds. Is it any business of yours, then, to get power or to be admitted in the entertainment industry? Of course not. How then, could this be discredit? And how could it be true that you will be a nobody everywhere when you should only be somebody in the things which are within your own power, in which you may be of the greatest importance? "But my friends will be unassisted." What do you mean by "unassisted"? They won't receive money from you, nor will you make them citizens of the country. Who told you, then, that these things are within our own power, and not really the affairs of others? And who can give to another person things which he himself doesn't possess? "Well, you say, what if I get them, then, we can share?" If you can get them with the preservation of your own honour and self-respect, show me the way you will get them; but if it requires you to lose your own goodness, so that you can gain what is not good, consider how unreasonable and foolish this is. Besides, which would you rather have, a sum of money or a faithful and honourable friend? Rather show me, then, how to gain this character than require me to do those things which may cause me to lose it. Well, but my country, say you, which depends upon me, will be unassisted. Here, again, what assistance is it that you mean? It will not have infrastructure, or public baths for use? And what indicates that? It is enough if everyone fully performs his own proper business. It will be supplied by another honourable citizen. Therefore, you do not need to declare yourself useless. So you ask, how should I help my country? Doing whatever you can do with consistency and honour. But if chose anything purely because you desire to be useful, and you lose these, how can you serve your country when you have become inconstant?

25

Do you find people who are preferred over you as entertainment, or given confidential information? If these things are good, you should be happy that he has them; and if they are evil, don't be upset that you don't have them. And remember that you cannot be expected to rival others in acquiring external praise or objects without using the same methods used to obtain them. How can a man who will not stand by the door of any man, will not accompany him, will not praise him, have an equal share to him who does these things? You are unreasonable, just like you would be unreasonable if you are unwilling to pay the price for these things if they were sold, and want to have them for nothing. How much are lettuces sold for? $1, for example. If another, then, pays $1, takes the lettuces, and you, haven't paid for it, don't think that he has gained an advantage over you. Because as he has the lettuce, but you have the $1 which you didn't give. So, in the present case, you haven't been recommended for entertainment because you haven't paid the price for which it is sold. It is sold for praise; it is sold for attendance. Give him, then, the value if it is in your favour to do so. But if you at the same time don't pay for something, and yet receive it, you are unreasonable and foolish.

26

The will of nature can be learned from viewing things which we all can agree on. Like when our neighbour's boy has broken a cup, or something similar, we are ready to say, "these type of things can and do happen"; be assured, then, that when your own cup is broken, you should act in the same wat as when another's cup is broken. Now apply this to greater things. Is the child or wife of another person dead? There is no one who wouldn't say, "This is unfortunately a part of life." But if anyone's own child happens to die, it is immediately, "Look what has happened to me!" It should be remembered always how we are affected when we hear the same thing affecting others.

27

A target is not set up for the sake of missing the aim, and neither is the nature of evil which exists in the world.

28

If a person had handed over your body to a stranger, you would certainly be angry. So why do you not feel any shame in handing over your own mind to any criticiser, to be unsettled and annoyed.

29

In every endeavour consider what comes before it and what follows, and then undertake it. Otherwise you will begin with spirit, of course, unaware of the consequences, and when these are developed, you will shamefully stop. "I want to conquer at the Olympic Games." But consider what precedes and what follows, and then, if it gives an advantage, pursue this. You must conform to rules, submit to a diet, refrain from treats; exercise your body, whether you choose it or not, at a stated hour, in hot and cold weather; you must drink no cold water, and sometimes no wine—in a word, you must give yourself up to your trainer. Then, in combat, you may be thrown onto the floor, dislocate your arm, twist your ankle, and, after all, lose the fight. When you have weighed this all up, if your inclination is to still train, go forward into combat. Otherwise, I'm warning you, you will behave like children who sometimes play as wrestlers, sometimes as gladiators, sometimes blow a trumpet, and sometimes act upset, when they mimic the shows they have admired. So you will also be at one time a wrestler, and another a gladiator; now a philosopher, now an orator; but nothing in resulting in sincere conviction. Like an ape you mimic all you see, and one thing after another pleases you, but comes out of your favour as soon as it becomes familiar to you. Because you have never started anything considerately; or after having researched and tested the subject, but carelessly, and with a half the energy. So, some, when they have seen a philosopher and heard a man speaking like Euphrates (because who can speak like him?)— then have a mind to be philosophers, as well. Therefore, consider first, what the subject really is, and what your own nature is able to bear. If you want to be a wrestler, consider your shoulders, your back, your thighs; because different people are made for different things. Do you think that you can act as you do and be a philosopher, that you can eat, drink, be angry, be discontented, as you are now? You must watch, you must work hard, you must conquer desires, must leave behind certain people, you may be despised, be laughed at by those you meet; come off worse than others in everything—at work, in honours, before tribunals. When you have fully considered all these things, approach, if you please—because by dealing with these things, you have a mind to purchase serenity, freedom, and tranquillity. If not, do not come here; do not, like children, be a philosopher now, then an orator, and then a soldier. These things are not consistent. You must be one man, either good or bad. You must cultivate either your own reason or else what the external gives you. You must apply yourself either to things inside you or outside you—that is, either be a philosopher or one of the crowd.

30

Duties are universally measured by relations. Is there a certain man you call your father? In this word it is implied you take care of him, and also submit to him in all things, patiently receiving his correction. But he is a bad father. Is your natural tie, then, to a *good* father? No, but to a father. Is a brother un reasonable? Well, preserve your own reasonable relation toward him. Don't consider what *he* does, but what *you* should do to keep your own will in a state conformable to nature, because another cannot hurt you unless you let them. You will only be hurt when you allow yourself to be hurt. In this manner, therefore, if you accustom yourself to contemplate the relations of your neighbours, citizens, commanders, you can conclude from each one what his or her corresponding duties are.

31

Understand that the essence of belief toward god lies in this—to form right opinions concerning god, as existing and as governing the universe fairly and well. And give yourself this resolution, to obey god, to yield to god, and willingly follow god among all events, being ruled by the most perfect wisdom. Because in this way you will never find fault with god, nor accuse god of neglecting you. And it is not possible for this to be affected in any other way than by withdrawing yourself from things which are not within our own power, and by believing good or evil to consist only in those which are. Because if you think any other things are either good or evil, it is inevitable that, when you are disappointed over that you wish for, or suffer from that which you wish to avoid, you shouldn't blame the author of the universe. Because every creature is naturally formed to run and regard with disgust the things that appear hurtful and that which causes them; and to pursue and admire those which appear beneficial and that which causes them. It is impossible, then, that someone who thinks he has been hurt should be happy about the person who, he thinks hurt him, just as it is impossible to be happy about the hurt itself. So, also, a father is criticized by his son when he does not impart the things which seem to be good; and this made Polynices and Eteocles mutually enemies—that empire seemed good to both. In this way the man criticizes god; the sailor, the merchant, or those who have lost a wife or child. Because where our interest is, there, too, our belief is directed. So whoever is careful to regulate his desires and aversions as he should do becomes careful of his beliefs also. But it also becomes necessary for everyone to offer sacrifices, according to the customs of his country, purely, and not negligently; not hoping for a greedy return, and not extravagantly.

32

When you require a source of help from god, remember that you won't know what the outcome will be, but through the outcome you will notice the divine; but the nature of the divine you should know about before the outcome; at least, if you have a philosophic mind. Because anything which isn't within our power can neither be good or evil. Do not, therefore, bring with you to god either desire or aversion—or else you are approaching god trembling—but first clearly understand that every event is indifferent and nothing to *you*, whatever kind it could be; because it will be in your power to make the right use of it, and this no one can deny. So go with confidence to god as your counselor; and afterwards, when any advice is given to you, remember what you have assumed, and what advice you will neglect if you disobey. Go to god as Socrates said, in cases which the whole consideration relates to the event, and which no deliberation is understood by reason. When, therefore, it is our duty to share the danger with a friend or with our country, we shouldn't consult god and ask whether we should share it with them or not. Because although god could warn you that the protection offered it unfavourable, this means no more than either death or mutilation or exile is possible. But we have reason within us; and it directs us, even with these hazards, to stand by our friend and our country. Remember, the great god, who once banished from the temple a man who neglected to save his friend.

33

Begin by assigning to yourself a good character and manner, so you feel balanced both alone and in the company of others.

Be silent as much as possible, and only speak about what is necessary, and in few words. We may, however, talk about other subjects for a little while sometimes, when the occasion calls for it; but don't let it be about any of the common subjects, like horse races, or athletic champions, or food, or drink—the meaningless topics of conversation—and not about men, especially to blame, praise, or make comparisons. If you are able to, during your own conversation, direct those in your company to proper subjects; but if you happen to find yourself among strangers, be silent.

Don't let your laughter be loud, frequent, or abundant.

Avoid making promises, if possible, altogether; at any rate, so far as you are able.

Avoid public and useless entertainment; but if an occasion brings you to them, keep your attention on something else important, so you won't unknowingly slide into indecency. Because be assured that if a person is pure, yet, if his companion is corrupted, he who converses with him will corrupted him also.

Provide what the body requires no more than what is absolutely necessary, such as meat, drink, clothing, shelter, advisors. But cut off everything that is only concerned with image and luxury.

Before marriage guard yourself with all your ability from sexual intercourse women; but don't mistreat or be severe with those who have been led into this, and don't boast frequently that you yourself do otherwise.

If anyone tells you that a certain person has spoken in a bad way about you, don't make excuses about what has been said, but answer: "He was ignorant of my other faults, otherwise he would have mentioned those also."

It is not necessary for you to appear often in public games; but if there is ever a proper occasion for you to be there, don't be more interested in anything other than yourself—that is, wish for things to be just as they are, and only the best man to win; because then nothing will go against you. Abstain entirely from cheering and ridiculing and violent emotions. And when you leave, don't talk a lot about what happened and what contributes nothing to your own benefit. Because it will only appear through your speech that you were dazzled by the show.

Avoid attending public speaking; but if you have to attend, preserve your seriousness and dignity, and also avoid making yourself disagreeable.

When you are going to consult with anyone, and especially with one who seems to be your superior, represent to yourself how Socrates or Zeno_would behave in a case like this, and you will make the most of the situation whatever may occur.

When you are going to visit anyone in power, think to yourself that you might not find him at home, that you may be shut out, that the doors may not be opened to you, that he may not notice you. If, with all this, it's your duty to go, bear what happens and never say to yourself, "It was not worth so much"; because this is disgraceful, and like a man confused by the external.

In the company of others, avoid frequent and excessive mentioning of your own actions and problems.

Because however agreeable it may be to yourself to allude to the risks you have, it is not equally agreeable to others to hear about your adventures. Avoid also any attempt to excite laughter, because this might make you appear distasteful, and, besides, it could also lower you in the esteem of your acquaintance. And any form of indecent conversation is also dangerous. Therefore, when anything like this happens, use the first opportunity to pull up anyone who makes advances like that in your direction, or, at least, by silence and a serious look show how displeased you are by talk like that.

34

If you are attracted by the resemblance of any promised pleasure, guard yourself against being affected by it; be patient and let this pass, and buy yourself some time. Then bring to your mind both points of time—the first when you will enjoy the pleasure, and then the time which you will regret and scold yourself, after contemplate a third option, in opposition to these, how you will rejoice and be proud of yourself if you abstain. And although it could appear to you as reasonable gratification, be cautious that its enticements and allurements and seductions could subdue you, so set in opposition to this how much better it is to be conscious of having gained a great a victory over yourself.

35

When you do anything with clear judgment that it should be done, never shrink from being seen to do it, even though the world could misunderstand it; because if you are not acting rightly, you should avoid the action; but if you are, why should you fear those who wrongly criticise you?

36

The saying, "it's either day or it's night," makes a lot of sense in an argument without a clear answer, but not in an argument which is already clear. Therefore, at dinner, to choose the largest share is only suitable to the bodily appetite, but not consistent with the social spirit of the entertainment. Remember, then, when you eat with another, don't only the value for the body the food which is set before you, but also value the proper courtesy toward your host.

37

If you are pretending to be a character beyond your strength, you have degraded your original self and quit being the character which you can support.

38

Just like walking you take care not to tread on a nail, or turn your foot outward, so also take care not to hurt the ruling faculty of your mind. And if we were to guard against this in every action, we will undertake any action more safely.

39

The body to everyone the measure of your fitness, therefore, if you stop exercise, you will stop where you were; and then be carried forward down a cliff; but if you go beyond your fitness level, you become gilded, and then studded with jewels. Because when one exceeds their measure of fitness there is no boundary.

40

Young women are flattered by men who give them the title of mistresses. They perceive that they are regarded as qualified to give men pleasure, they then begin to beautify themselves, and in beauty they place all their hopes. It is worthwhile, therefore, to try and perceive themselves as honoured only so far as they appear beautiful in their appearance and modestly virtuous.

41

It is the sign of the intellect to not spend too much time in things relating to the body, less time spent on exercise, eating and drinking, and any of the other animal functions. These things should be done incidentally, and our main strength should be applied to our reason.

42

When any person does wrong to you, or speaks in a bad way about you, remember that he is acting or speaking from an impression that it's right for him to do so. It isn't possible that he would follow what appears right to you, but only what appears right to himself. Therefore, if he judges you on a false appearance, he is the person who is hurt, because he is the person that has been deceived. Because, if anyone takes to be true what is false about another, the accused isn't hurt, only the accuser who has been deceived. So, from these principles, you have to bear with people who dislike you, because you can say about every occasion, "It appears that way to him."

43

Everything has two handles: one by which it can be carried, another by which it can't. If your brother acts unfairly, don't hold the handle of his injustice, because by that it cannot be carried, but rather by the opposite—that he is your brother, that he was brought up with you; and that you will hold on to the handle which it can be carried by.

44

Statements like these have no logical connection: "I am richer than you, therefore I am your superior." "I am more eloquent than you, therefore I am your superior." The true logical connection is actually this: "I am richer than you, therefore my possessions exceed yours." "I am more eloquent than you, therefore my style must surpass yours." But we, after all, consist neither in property nor in style.

45

For anyone who bathes in a rush, don't say that he is ill, but he is hasty. For anyone who drinks a lot of wine, don't say that he is ill, but that he drinks a lot. Because unless you perfectly understand his motives, how do you know if he is ill? So you shouldn't risk judging any appearances, unless you fully comprehend them.

46

Never declare yourself to be a philosopher, or talk a lot with the ignorant about your principles, but show them by actions. And, in social settings, don't tell people how they should eat, but eat as you should. Because remember that Socrates also universally avoided all pretentiousness. And when people came to him and desired to be introduced by him to philosophers, he took them and introduced them; his actions were seen and not spoken, and no one failed to overlook him. So if you're ever among the ignorant during any discussion of principles, be as silent as you can. Because there is great danger in throwing out what is undigested. And if anyone tells you that you know nothing, and you are not irritated by it, then you can be sure that you have really begun your work. Because even sheep don't throw up the grass to show the shepherds how much they have eaten, but, inwardly digesting their food, they produce it outwardly in wool and milk. Therefore, don't make an exhibition before the ignorant about your principles, but show the actions which the digestion of principles creates.

47

When you have learned to nourish your body frugally, don't feel irritated by it; nor, if you drink water, say after every occasion, "I only drink water." First consider how much more frugal you are than even the poor, and how much more patient of hardship. If at any time you inure yourself by exercise and a lack of food, for your own sake and not for the public, don't attempt miracles here; when you are violently thirsty, drink as much as you need.

48

The condition and characteristic of a disgusting person is that doesn't look internally how he can help or how he harms himself, but only what he can acquire externally. The condition and characteristic of a philosopher is that he looks internally for how he harms himself and then how he can help himself. The characteristics of a proficient man are that he scolds no one, praises no one, blames no one, accuses no one; says nothing concerning himself about being somebody or knowing anything. When he is hindered or restrained, he accuses himself; and if he is praised, he smiles to himself at the person who praises him; and if he is attacked, he makes no defence. But he goes about with caution, careful of interference with anything that is doing well but not yet quite secure. He restrains desire; he transfers his avoidance to those things only which art the proper use of his own will; he employs his energies moderately in all directions;

if he appears stupid or ignorant, he does not care; and, ultimately, he keeps watch over himself – like watching an enemy.

49

When anyone shows himself as vain on being able to understand and interpret the works of Chrysippus, say to yourself: "Unless Chrysippus had written obscurely, this person has nothing to be vain about. What do I desire? To understand nature, and follow it. I ask, then, who interprets nature; and hearing that Chrysippus does, I have to follow him. I don't understand his writings. I seek, therefore, someone to interpret *them*." So far there is nothing to value about myself in this situation. And when I find an interpreter, what remains I need to make use of his instructions. This alone is the valuable thing. But if I admire the interpretation only, then what do I become more than a grammarian, instead of a philosopher. Then when anyone asks me to read Chrysippus to him, I would blush when I cannot read the text in a harmonious way.

50

Whatever rules you have adopted, respect them as if they were laws, and as if you would be prosecuted if you go against them; and don't regard what anyone says about you, because this, after all, is no concern of yours. How long, then, could you delay to demand from yourself improvement, and in no instance to go against your judgments derived from reason? You have received the philosophic principles with which you should to be familiar with. So, what other master, then, do you wait for, as an excuse to delay your self-reformation? You are no longer a boy but a grown man. If, therefore, you are negligent and slothful, and always add procrastination to procrastination, purpose to purpose, and say day after day that you will attend to yourself, you will insensibly continue to accomplish nothing, and when living and dying, continue to possess a disgusting mind. This instant, then, think to yourself that you are worthy of living as a man, grown up and proficient. Let whatever appears to be the best to you an inviolable law. And if any instance of pain or pleasure, glory or disgrace, is in front of you, remember that now is the time to fight, it cannot be put off; and that by one failure and defeat your honour could be lost or—won. Socrates became perfect, improving himself in everything, following his reason. And although you are not yet like Socrates, you should, however, live as someone seeking to be like Socrates.

51

The first and most necessary topic in philosophy is the practical application of principles, *not to lie*; the second is the demonstrations, *why we shouldn't lie*; the third, the one which gives strength and logical connection to the other two, is, *why this is a demonstration*. Because what is a demonstration? What is a consequence? What is a contradiction? What is truth? What is a lie? The third point is then necessary to make the second clear; and the second to make the first clear. But the most necessary, and that more important that the rest, is the first. But sometimes people do the opposite. Because they spend all the time on the third point and use their diligence around that, and entirely neglect the first. Therefore, at the same time that we lie, we are very ready to show how it can be demonstrated that lying is wrong.

On all occasions we should have these sayings ready:

Control me god, toward my destiny,

> To wherever you have fixed my destination.

I follow cheerfully; and, if I don't,

> In sad manner, I have to follow anyway.

Whoever properly understands fate is deemed

> Wise among men, and knows the laws of Heaven.

And this also:

"If it pleases god, let it be."

"They may kill me; but they cannot hurt me".

END

For more adapted classics by James Harris please visit:

Http://ViewAuthor.at/JamesHarris

Printed in Great Britain
by Amazon